Fletch Chomped

by Faith Sherlock
illustrated by Rémy Simard

Practice Decodable 36

I0806513

McGraw Hill Education

Bothell, WA • Chicago, IL • Columbus, OH • New York, NY

MHEonline.com

McGraw-Hill Education

Send all inquiries to:
McGraw-Hill Education
8787 Orion Place
Columbus, OH 43240

ISBN: 978-0-02-137154-9
MHID: 0-02-137154-7

Printed in China.

8 9 10 11 12 DSS 27 26 25 24 23

Crunch! Crunch!

Fletch chomped and chomped.

Fletch munched plastic latches.

"Pass that batch of tacks," he said.

Fletch gulped down branches.
Fletch had chopped-up rugs.

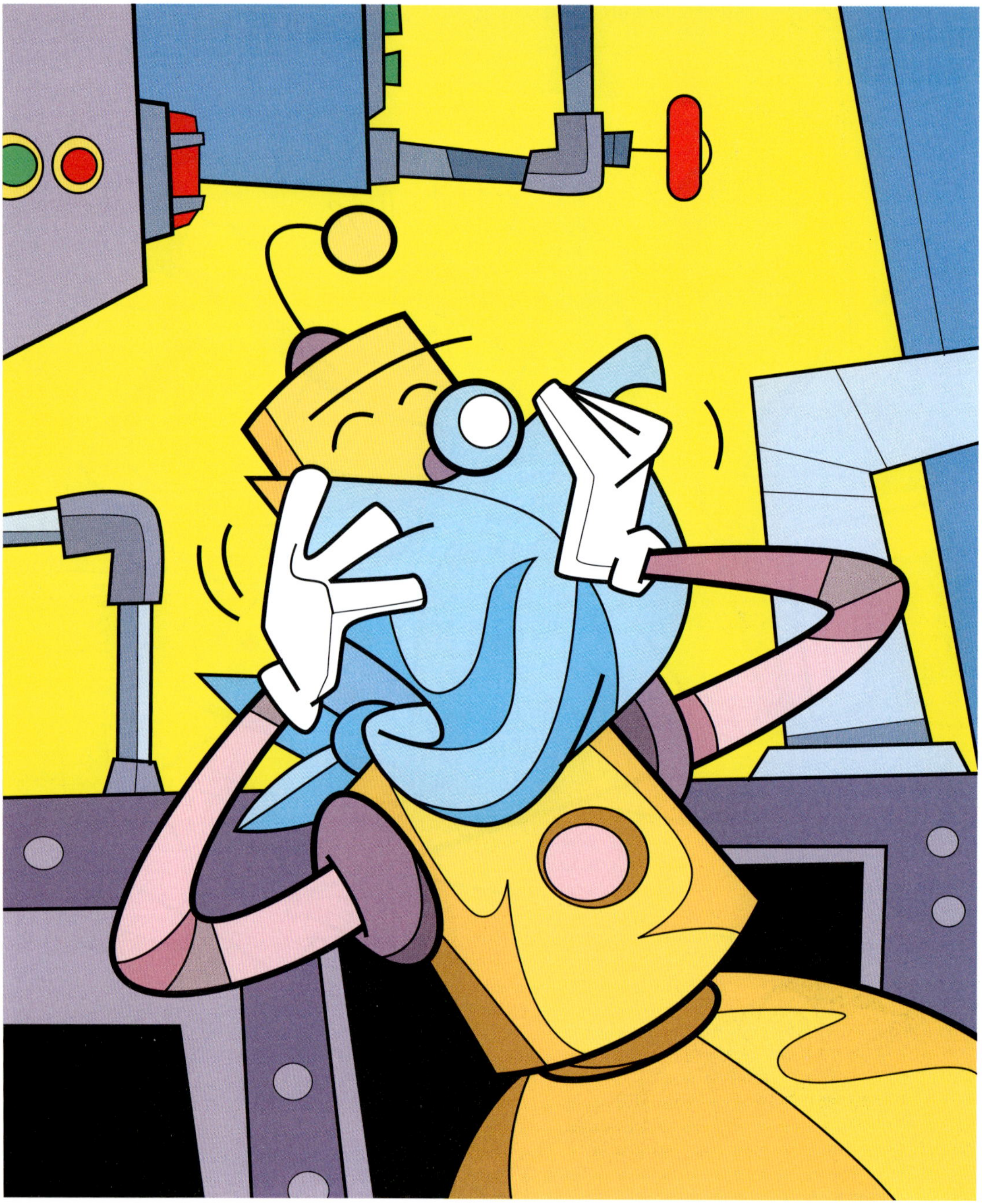

Fletch brushed his chin.

He munched his napkin!

Fletch got up.

Then he chomped down his bench!

"That was the best snack," said Fletch.
"Let's have lunch!"